Praise for Ed Meek's HIGH TIDE

***

In "On the Outer Cape in August," meteorites are "flaming out like dreams at dawn." In "Hunting Mushrooms with Mina," "stars colonize the Big Sky." When Ed Meek isn't looking up, he's noticing the "Asian woman - all angles," playing "Paint It Black" "underneath the street" on her violin as the train approaches the station, and he thinks of all the "artists, musicians, poets" we'll never notice or even know of, unless we're paying attention, even when we're waiting for the train.

Is it an overstatement to suggest that one function of poetry is to help us learn to see? When the subject is Ed Meek's work, I think it's a simple fact.

—Bill Littlefield
Author of *Prospect* and *Take Me Out*
Host of NPR's *Only a Game*

Ed Meek's poems pull us in with such clarity that you don't feel the pain at first, almost like a painting you need to study until you see what's waiting in the shadows, that scarred figure, its history.

—Nina Rubinstein Alonso
Editor of *Constellations*, a Journal of Poetry and Fiction

If you are hungry for a fine feast of poetry, Ed Meek will fill your plate with delicious poems. His newest poetry book is a trifecta of lyric, narrative, and nature poems. In "How to Make Meatballs," the end product is not what one would expect. In "Miss Maloney," fifth grade tough guys set out to break a teacher. Every poem in this carefully crafted volume is well worth reading. Who could ask for more?

—Zvi A. Sesling
Brookline, MA Poet Laureate
Editor and Publisher of *Muddy River Poetry Review*
Author of *War Zones* and *The Lynching of Leo Frank*

Other Books by Ed Meek

Flying
What We Love
Spy Pond
Luck: Stories

HIGH TIDE

Ed Meek

Aubade Publishing
Ashburn, VA

Copyright © 2020 Ed Meek

All rights reserved. No part of this publication may be reproduced, stored in a retrieval system, or transmitted in any form or by any means, electronic, mechanical, photocopying, recording, or otherwise, without the prior written permission of Aubade Publishing.

Edited by Joe Puckett

Cover and book design by Cosette Puckett

Library of Congress Control Number: 2020930661

ISBN: 978-1-951547-99-8

Published by Aubade Publishing, Ashburn, VA

Printed in the United States of America

To Elizabeth

Only that day dawns to which we are awake.

> — Henry David Thoreau

It's bad out there. High waters everywhere.

> —Bob Dylan

Contents

Hammock	1
Junkyard of Broken Dreams	2
Hunting Mushrooms with Mina	3
Welcome to Laundry Town	5
Food Town	6
The Lottery	7
The Crossing Guard	8
Pi	9
Sigh	10
Angel Falls	11
Talking Trees	12
Downy Woodpecker	13
Pinch Me	14
Kiss	15
Praise for Ponytailed Girls Who Run	17
High Tide	18
For My Mother	19
Nine First Fridays	20
The Price of Heat	21
The Black Paintings	22
The Maid Pouring Milk	23
Christ Mocked by the Soldiers	24
Limbo	25
Remote Control	26
Talking to Yourself	27
Powder Blue	28
The Poetry Motel	30
Death to Poetry!	31
Advertisement Paid for by the Poets for American Expression PAC	32
In the Poetry Motel	33
March	34
November in New England	35
At the Well	36
Drifting Home	37
Sail Away	38

Contents

Dumb Luck	39
Make America Great Again	41
Pilloried	43
Identify	44
Whipping Boy	46
How to Make Meatballs	47
Miss Maloney	48
Idling	50
Old Enemies	51
Call to the Furies	53
American Dream	54
American Elegy	55
Gypsy Moth	56
Encomium for the God of Nothingness	57
Ex-Nuns	58
Baker's Chocolate	59
Social Security	60
In the Dead of Winter in Somerville	61
The Tropical Forest in Franklin Park	62
Royal Rendezvous in August	63
Heron	64
Curveball	65
Riding	66
Lava	67
We Support Our Troops	68
So Many Men	69
Funeral at Sea	70
Summer in Wellfleet	71
Cahoon Hollow	72
Something's Not Right	73
Nevertheless	74
Ghost Bikes	75
On the Train	77
The Last Game	78
On the Outer Cape	79

HIGH TIDE

Hammock

Mayans carved them from the bark of trees
Columbus noted in his diary.
Later, sailors tied them
beneath the deck
to roll with the waves.
Now my son hitches one
between the trees
when he camps with friends.
While each June I hook the hammock
his high school flame
gave us as a gift
to two pitch pines
in the back yard.
It's a promise of long afternoons
of shaded naps in the sun.
A promise I usually fail to keep.
But now I'm sixty-five with a little more time
on my hands, I swing late
some days into the latticed rope
and hang suspended above the earth
like a spider in a web. There I dream
of camping trips I never took with friends
and sailors I might have met
in a different life on the open seas
and Mayans half asleep
when Columbus washed ashore.

Junkyard of Broken Dreams

—For Richard Hugo

The driveway displays
a late-model muscle car
up on blocks
and a scaffold harbors
a dilapidated boat,
paint peeling, motor
missing parts. Where
a yard once was
scraps of wood crush the weeds—
watch out for nails!
The garage hides reclaimed chairs,
legless tables, burnt-out lamps,
discarded notes, Styrofoam coffee cups,
broken bats, duck-taped hockey sticks.
You can't give this stuff away.
Wouldn't that mean giving up?
This is where he'll make his last stand,
fight the losing battle till the bitter end.
"I'll drink to that!" he crows
and laughs as he fires a dead soldier
into the bow of the boat.
Listen: you can hear the glass shatter from here
in this junkyard of broken dreams.

Hunting Mushrooms with Mina

I went hunting morels with my Sioux friend Mina.
We took her Mustang GT into the woods outside Missoula.
When the fire road ended we got out to forage.
She was my eyes and knew where to look.
I was along for the ride. She lifted leaves
and poked through thatch
to find them crouching in damp quarters,
secreted in moss and duff. They were
long-dead shrunken dwarfs
buried in their hats, their bodies
a stump beneath their shaggy, fetid heads.
They'd wept for years and moist riverbeds
coursed down their spongy faces.

"What about these?" I asked
pointing to a yellow disk, speckled with white freckles.
"Death cap," she said. "I can poison you with that."
Her long black hair reflected light and my eye
caught the tip of the blade
she kept on her hip.

We ferried our mushrooms to her cabin
just south of town. With garlic, butter, and salt
they were savory as meat.
They stood up
to the grilled loin of the deer
she'd taken with her bow
and butchered with her knife.

"What do you think?" she asks.
"I'm wondering how we won."
"Germs and guns," she says.
 Outside we share a pipe
 while the moon silvers her hair
 and stars colonize the Big Sky.
"Teach me your ways," I say.

Welcome to Laundry Town

If you are a little down
on your luck—divorced, thrown out,
foreclosed—you just might find yourself
lugging the wash to Laundry Town
where the change machine
charges 10% and you need to scrape
handfuls of lint off the filter
to make the dryer work.
Keep in mind detergent
costs extra and the water
in the washers never gets hot.
Don't forget to keep an eye
on your clothes after you fold them
and don't think for a minute
you can run next door to Food Town
for a salty snack while the machines spin.
You'll come back to find your favorite jeans,
the Nike sweats, and your warm wool socks
MIA, and no one there
saw a damn thing.
But wait, here they are after all,
worn and rumpled, like you,
at the bottom of the pile
in the lost and found.

Food Town

You only stop at Food Town
as a last resort. Half-empty shelves
stocked with pork rinds, chips,
and beef jerky. The milk expired
days ago. There's a sale
on half-gallon jugs of Mountain Dew.
A bottle spilled and the floor's so sticky
your shoes squelch as you walk.
The clerk, a refugee From Uganda,
appears underage. He must have won
the lottery and ended up here—
seven days a week at minimum wage.
He says he rooms with a distant aunt,
takes classes online in code
and wires money home.
"I'm lucky," he says. "In six months,
robbed just once!" His smile
flashes in the dim light
of the dingy store.

The Lottery

In another version of reality
I get a low number in the draft.
I go into the Marines
like my father and my brother.

I make it to Khe Sanh in 1968
where I save John Smith.
Not Pocahontas's Captain,
but John Smith of Milton, Mass.,
the center on my football team
who hiked the ball between his legs
to my open hands. I drop back

from my platoon and see a VC
zero in on John. I raise my M1,
fire and miss, and the gook
disappears. "John," I call,
"it's me, Ed!" Instead,

I drew a high number
in the draft.
I won the lottery
and lost my center.

The Crossing Guard

1

You can't miss the crossing guard—
that luminescent lemon drop
at the corner each day.
He waits with the patience of Job
ready to perform his sacred duty.

With hands as old as vines twisted by time
he holds the divine red lollypop—
its simple command in four black letters.
When he raises his arm, bikes, cars, and trucks
like well-trained soldiers grind to a halt
as he ferries the children across the dangerous divide.

2

He'll be there at the river to help us on board,
hold the ferry steady when the wind picks up,
or the currents are strong.
Are you ready? He'll ask smiling—
the last words we'll remember
as we embark and watch the shore fade away
before we turn to face the wind
and whatever lies ahead.

Pi

You hold the answer to the question:
Why study math? See
for yourself, you say.
Yet you remain inscrutable,
impossible to pin down,
infinite in your wisdom.

Say I pace the circumference
of a kettle pond. Then swim
straight across. Will that
get me to you?

The Egyptians thought one-third;
the Greeks cracked your code.
Now we know you're always right.
Size doesn't matter!
Still you're irrational
like someone who keeps
changing the subject,
yet everything she says
is true.

Sigh

It's a relief sometimes.
this single note,
from a forgotten song
carried by breath
like a wave by wind.

It escapes unintentionally
before you can stop it
causing you pause

between thoughts
or at the tail end
of a moment—

an afterthought
or a prelude
or an afterword—

a giveaway
or maybe a clue
to life
or death.

Isn't that last exhale
a sigh—
the wave dissipating
on an unknown shore . . .

Angel Falls

> "No man steps into the same river twice."
> —Heraclitus

I keep stepping into the same river
over and over again. Sometimes
I slip and fall in. Usually,
it's cold, but not always.
It's deep enough to swim
and I do. Upstream, of course,
fighting against the current,
just like Fitzgerald said,
but finding my own rhythm—
totally immersed—three strokes
then catch some air—
often getting nowhere fast.
Nonetheless, I swim on
and find the shore
just before the waterfall.
I'm not going through that again!

Talking Trees

The rumors are true—it's a fact.
They've been talking all along—
above our heads, behind our backs
beneath our feet. Now we know
what mushrooms do with their silly caps
and fetid roots. We've heard the trees
whispering as we walk, on the surface,
in our own little world, oblivious as usual;
where the real action is way down deep
where we cannot see what's going on.
Yet we've long known that they were here
before we arrived and will survive
after we're gone: redwood, oak,
baobab, pine. Admit it, they're divine!

Downy Woodpecker

You too must tire of the clatter
of your own beak, rebounding
off the bark of the oak
and sticking to the pitch pine.

I assumed in search of grubs
and other yucky bugs
but they are only half the story.

What really matters to you—
communication. This is where you are
and what you have to say.

Your song—all percussion.
No tattletale, you announce yourself,
blow your own horn
in shameless self-promotion.

Shake your rattle!
Let it be known:
You're in the market for love.

Pinch Me

Pinch me, doll, I can't believe it's real.
Is it what you think, or what you feel?
Am I wrong? Is it all just lies?
Or is romance really faith in disguise?
It's your heart I was meant to steal.
Don't think about it; go with what you feel.
Do we ever really know when it is real?
Sometimes you have to get right down and kneel.
That's right, we all believe in lies.
Romance is just faith in disguise.
Face it, Ed, you've lost sight of what is real.
Forget about what you think; it's what you feel.

Kiss

I'm thinking of a kiss
from years ago—
probably better remembered
than experienced
I don't know
but I swear
I remember
a sort of
meltdown
emanating
from deep
in the heart
of the brain—
a sort of reverse
volcano. Suddenly
on alert,
the nerves
of the skin
abuzz
with anticipation,
the unspoken dialogue
of desire
requiring
mouth-to-mouth
resuscitation.
Our bodies wired—
alive with current:
we were plugged in—
electrons dancing
to an unnamed tune

carried on waves
of light,
bending time
and space,
until we couldn't
take anymore
and disengaged.

Praise for Ponytailed Girls Who Run

I love to see them bouncing past
on the balls of their feet—
hair pulled back to flaunt
flawless skin, flashing
arms from T-shirts, legs
in short shorts, multi-colored,
incandescent shoes.

They've reconstructed beauty,
these young girls
with their modest breasts,
legs defined by muscle,
peachy, callipygian butts . . .

And the hair, lovely,
surely not dead
but vibrant with life and light
as it sways and bobs
like a rope swing in the wind
above the water.

High Tide

When I was young, the two of them were young too.
At the beach at Brant Rock,
my father, handsome and strong,
with his Elvis Presley hair
and Icelandic-blue eyes, my mother,
slim and pretty with her majorette
legs and perfectly cultivated tan.

My father held me up
in the water and my mother
waved from her beach blanket
on the sand. This was before
my brother and sisters, those
uninvited guests, crashed
the party, back when my mother
was fun to be around
and my father was glad
to be home from the war,
working the only job
he would ever have.

Before we left we'd weave along
the shore, heads down
in search of shells.
I walked between them—
one on each hand. The three of us
happy as clams at high tide.

For My Mother

She could be fun
with the whimsicality
of a leaf
held aloft by wind,
buoyant as a boat,
happily rudderless,
drifting beneath
a sunny sky.

She loved a sunny sky
and a sunny disposition—
thought them prerequisites
for a successful life,
which may be why
she was depressed—
disapproving of the serial divorces
of my sisters
and the estranged, overly sensitive son
who ran away to the Maine woods
and never came back.

But I see I've tacked off course.
I wanted to give praise
to her smile—
its sunny warmth
and the effort it took
to don daily
no matter which way
the wind blew.

Nine First Fridays

When I was thirteen I made
the nine First Fridays. My mother
coaxed me out of bed before school
with the promise of eternal life.
We braved the dark cold
of New England winter
for 7:00 a.m. Mass at Saint Agatha's.

There we waltzed station to station
following the trail of Jesus
who bore the heavy wooden cross
the Romans would nail him to
before he rose triumphant to heaven.
I was already plagued like Saint Thomas
by doubt. My mother kept me
close at hand. An Irish Catholic
who loved to gamble—
bingo every Monday,
chances are she'd find
the gates unlocked. I was
another story. We were both
hedging our bets.

The Price of Heat

When the coal rumbled down the chute
into the cellar bin, black dust rose
in clouds that hovered
like a murder of crows.

My father shoveled bituminous rocks
into the open mouth of the squat
iron furnace, the flames glowing
with the fire of an underground sun.
I was only three, too young to help,
but old enough to see.

When we trudged upstairs
the dust trailed us like smoke
to settle in the curtains, napkins,
and tablecloths my mother washed
and ironed each week.

She stood at the top of the stairs,
one hand on her hip,
the other pointing to the kitchen sink
where the bar of lye soap sat.
Her granddad had worked the mines in England.
She knew the price of heat.

The Black Paintings

"Silence is so accurate."
—Mark Rothko

An irrational impulse in a rational form, Nietzsche said. Or is it a rational impulse in an irrational form? We make sense of it: like a disaster, a suicide.

The joke's on us: anybody could do that! You could do that.

The artist expressing how he felt at a particular moment in time: 3:00 a.m. in winter.

He was depressed. He was beyond depression.

He was searching in the darkness
for the inner light.
He found gradations of black,
from flat to pitch to pearl,
from dusk to night—
the opposite of blindness
which can be white.

The work speaks for itself. Mum's the word.

The Maid Pouring Milk

Vermeer knew the secret of light—
how it can illuminate
a life, sweeping majestically
like a halcyon broom,

the sun transmutes a loaf of bread
into gold, turns a dull scarf
royal blue and transforms
a maid pouring milk
into a work of art.

As if to say, from a certain angle
at just the right time of day
light imbues our lives,
no matter who we are,
with undeniable beauty.

Christ Mocked by the Soldiers

Rouault's Christ is sad but resilient.
He refuses to answer his captors
who taunt him as if they are in
on a joke, as if they know

who he is—just another
phony prophet. Yet he remains
true to his vision—he takes
the long view, ignoring

the pain, the blood, steeling himself
for what he knows will come:
thorny crown, blunt nails,
long hours on the cross

waiting for the wings
that will fly him home.

Limbo

— Erthe Toc of Erthe (Anonymous ca 1000, England)

"You are a dime a dozen," my superior said.
She didn't mean to be mean.
She only wanted to set me straight on the job market—
a simple matter of supply and demand.

Erthe toc of erthe erthe wyth woh,

There are too many good people like you available—
what she meant: not dime a dozen.
"I didn't mean to imply you have no value," she added.

erthe other erthe to the erthe droh,

She just meant to be honest—
let me know where I stood—
the reason she couldn't hire me.
She knew exactly what it was like to be in my position.
She had worked part-time herself.

erthe leyde erthe in erthene throh

As a woman had to work twice as hard
to get to where she is now.
She merely wanted me to know it wasn't her fault;

tho hevede erthe of erthe erthe ynoh.

she didn't have a say in the matter.
She was a victim of the system
just like everyone else.

Remote Control

It was 3:00 a.m. I lay in bed, so tired I couldn't sleep. In fact, my mind was spinning with all I had to do in the coming days, weeks, and years. There wasn't enough time, really, when you thought about it, to get things done so I got up to make a list. As I was doing so, I began to remember all I hadn't yet accomplished, until the list of unfinished and yet-to-be-undertaken projects lay like a yoke across my shoulders. It was a yoke I had to get out from under, so I took down the bottle of bourbon from the cabinet and poured myself a drink.

    I took the bottle downstairs and turned on the TV and sat with the remote in one hand, drink in the other, intermittently pushing the plus or minus channel button, jumping from one program to another, impatient to find something worthwhile to watch, bored with reruns, ads, talk shows, news. I didn't have time for this, I thought, pouring myself another bourbon, fingering the remote.

Talking to Yourself

It's no big deal. "It still could work out," you say. You're talking to yourself. It won't work out and it reminds you of everything else wrong—all you failed to finish, corners cut, bad decisions. Now life isn't anywhere near what it's supposed to be, what they said it'd be, how you thought it would turn out, and you notice, there at the kitchen table, depression sits—gray all over—eyes like lead. You feel a chill. You must have left the door open—when you weren't looking he slipped in.

Suddenly you're weak—dizzy with regret. "Sit down," he says, and you find yourself staring across the table at his flat, lifeless eyes. You can't get up, can't look away, you're uncomfortable in your own skin, like a dog in a drought—if you could move, you'd get a drink or take a bath. Your throat so dry you can't swallow. You can't swallow it all anymore, the strangers who occupy your house—your wife and children—as distant as the relatives who raised you. You knew them all once, long ago, in another country you called home.

There are pills that could help. If you had the energy you'd take them. But you can't take them...don't want... can't think straight here in conditional country—the marsh of maybe, miasma of would, could, if only, might, would, should have. Your tongue has turned to sand. Your thoughts are not your own. You can't trust yourself.

Powder Blue

The poet Richard Hugo once told me
he wanted a Mercedes—
powder blue. I scoffed,
then thought of his arthritic knees,
blackened lungs, dysfunctional liver—
thirty years of cigarettes and booze.
He'd fought the last World War,
worked fifteen years at Boeing;
he deserved a nice ride.
That was forty years ago. Today
I bought a BMW,
titanium paint, xenon headlights,
moonroof, seventeen-inch
alloy wheels.

What did I do
to deserve this? Was I born
at the right time, here
in North America—
far from Al-Qaeda's caves,
minefields, hand-held missiles?
Don't I deserve to be scammed
by the venal salesman whose boss
pads the sticker with add-ons?
Wouldn't you like to vandalize my car,
gleaming in the driveway?

Say you were Arabic, pious
in your prayers to Allah,
your country run by

two-faced lackeys.
Wouldn't you love
to fly to America,
all expenses paid,
to place a plastic explosive
beneath the wheel of my car
and watch it blow
on the nightly news,
me in it?

The Poetry Motel

When you check in it's early or late depending on your point of view which changes periodically when you're not looking. Just now for instance, carrying your one bag to the room with a view. Moments ago, on the highway, you were dead tired behind the wheel of the late model sports sedan which you insist on keeping on the road against your better judgment. You were nodding in and out of consciousness—reality a place you returned to out of a sense of duty. You could have fallen asleep to crash into a tree just like that; or you could have found a rest area and conked in the car, but you wanted to make the next exit so you'd have the feeling you had gotten somewhere. And when you finally did pull into the parking lot of the motel, it was quiet—the only light the blinking neon sign—you had to knock and ring the office bell a number of times until the old woman finally answered and grudgingly gave you the key. "Pay later," she said and smiled as if there was more to it than that.

    When you found your room, you turned the key; the lock tumbled and you went in and flicked the switch. It wasn't exactly what you wanted, but it wasn't bad either. You sat on the bed and the old springs sang. You drew the drapes and sure enough—a view of the mountains—hazy blue in the distance, peaks lost in white mist. You had been here before you felt suddenly, as the first rays of sunlight cut through the haze.

Death to Poetry!

"Painting disgusts me. I want to assassinate painting."
— Joan Miró

Poetry disgusts me—its cowardly retreat
from life, its incestuous relations,
the fetid pools . . . the shallow unprofound
schools, the shameless self-promotion,
its blah, blah blurbs,
its thin-skinned fear
of criticism. I want
to assassinate poetry,
with a bullet to the brain
a coup d'état . . .

or we could blow it up
with a percussion bomb
so loud it echoes
through the halls of academia.

Let heads roll
from the guillotines.
I want to see poetry
bleeding in the streets.
We will bury the dead
in a mass grave.
Let the revolution begin!

Advertisement Paid for by the Poets for American Expression PAC

Does your life lack focus?
Have your batteries run down, a charger nowhere in sight?
Confused about priorities? Enveloped in ennui?

Talk to your doctor about poetry.
It can imbue your life with metaphor
And lift your spirits like a drone.

Side effects include: red-rimmed eyes,
waning interest in television,
the need to prostrate oneself while reading,
vast quantities of red wine,
restless nights,
hot flashes of insight,
puzzling dreams,
flights of whimsy,
unexpected naps,
delinquent daydreams,
odysseys in light rain,
an unhealthy obsession with language,
love of the sound of certain words:
susurrations, palpable, insouciant.

Poetry could be the cure you're looking for.
Talk to your doctor about poetry.

In the Poetry Motel

The clerk gives you the key to your room. You have your doubts but keep them to yourself. At the far end of the corridor you turn the key. It's a standard room: single bed, chair, desk, and bible. You take a seat to clear your head and write. You hear in the back of your ear a faint strain of music—something so familiar. It seems to be coming from the back of the room. Then you notice another door.
    You try the key and it opens. A radio on the desk is playing the music you heard. In the corner in the shadows someone sits. She beckons with a crooked finger, come closer. She has something to tell you. You bend down to listen. She is old and frail. She whispers in a foreign tongue. It could be Latin or Greek. You seem to know some of the words. When she waves you off you return to the desk in your room. You try to make sense of it.

March

In New England, March hangs on to winter
like an old overcoat it won't throw away.

Yet March longs for change, throws open
the windows for a deep breath
of cool, green air.

March is bipolar:
Cold one day; warm the next.

In March snow turns to rain
and ruins the ice.
Rivers run off
and overflow their banks.

And March makes mud slides—
watch your step! Meanwhile

March is impatient, leaning
forward, tapping its foot,
ready to spring.

November in New England

Your chosen colors brown and gray
keep you somber as a sober drunk.

On your watch, leaves
lose their luster and once they fall,
turn to clutter—slippery as eels
beneath our feet.

The skeletal branches of trees
map the sky with dead ends.
The sun cold as gold, a distant
cousin we seldom see.

Being next to last has made you bitter.
You are the wake
before the funeral of December.

At the Well

On a crisp April morning you walk out to the well,
bucket in hand. As you walk the bucket swings.
You take care not to let it bruise your hip. It is heavy,
old and worn—the metal frame has cut you before
and once, the band broke, the bucket fell apart,
and you had to glue it back together piece by piece.

At the well you hook the handle to the rope
and lower the bucket down into the darkness—
you make a circle with your fingers
and the rope slides through.

Years ago you had only to dip the bucket
just below the surface of the earth and it came back brimming,
but each year you have to lower the bucket more.
Now you find yourself at the end of your rope
so you lean over the well and reach down.
You hear the water bubbling into the bucket
and you begin to pull it up hand over hand.
It is much heavier than you expected
and you are suddenly overcome by exhaustion.

Drifting Home

At the end of the corridor of noise
you know the voice of the clock
is an echo in a vacuum
and what's lost hangs like a broken door.

Somewhere in the desert of all that is left undone
hopes and dreams gather—old friends.
Some bring water, others carry reptiles.
On one's shoulder, a lyre sings.

But it is your mother the ocean
who drifts in waves in your sleep
and years pass by in a dream. The Sioux
called this the shadow world.

Somehow, we forget the simplest things.
How dreams carry us in a boat
from this world to that and back
unharmed until you wake one night

drifting just offshore—everyone
you thought you lost, friends
and lovers smile, Welcome.

Sail Away

Five thousand years ago
Mesopotamian square sails
propelled boats
as long as the wind lasted.
Egyptians added oars
manned by slaves
to take up the slack.
Arabs rigged their sails
to split the wind, tack and jibe,
while Vikings molded the hull with a keel
that cut waves down to size.

These boats were the bridges
that connected the dreams
of civilizations—
old worlds and new . . .

Today to sail means to dream
of leaving land behind
to skim the surface of the water
like flying fish.

Dumb Luck

Three times Bobby stole cars and totaled them.
The first time, drunk, not yet an alcoholic,
he was the all-star guard
who rallied Milton with jump shots, floaters
and coast to coast layups.
The cop who found him
unconscious, slumped over the wheel,
phoned his old man—
the mechanic who kept their cars running.
Sowing wild oats, they said—
a joy ride, no one hurt.
Except maybe the tree, they joked.

The second time was the limit—
the Cadillac wrapped around a telephone pole.
No more favors, the officer
who dropped him off said.
Nine lives, the old man quipped
and cuffed Bobby's unscratched head.

Third time was messy.
The cops who yanked him from the wreck
rushed him to the hospital.
He had to file a report.
And the old man had to replace
the car. Lucky it belonged
to an old customer.

The scars on Bobby's face would remind him
of the lesson he failed to learn.
Everything happens in threes

His mother said when he died
from his third heart attack.

Make America Great Again

Let's take America back
to the straitjacket
of the 1950s—
when women knew
their place
and cops let
domestic abuse
slide, divorcees
were outcast
and the church
lied for priests
who brought altar boys
to their knees
while teachers and coaches
were given
a good talking to
or a year off
if they took advantage
of their boys and girls,
and gay kids
were routinely
beaten by macho guys
and mental illness
was cause for shame,
the retarded, objects
of ridicule.
The good old days
when no women
or Jews were allowed,

Blacks were happier
with their own kind
and America could do
no wrong.

Pilloried

> "Basket of deplorables."
>
> —Hillary Clinton,
> 2016 presidential campaign

It was a basket of rotten apples
we carried with us on our trek home.
It was a Pandora's casket of irredeemables.

We had a dream today
but it was deplorable, abhorrent, horrific,
laden with adjectives that had been nouned:
terribles, horribles, awfuls.

Like nouns that had been verbed,
we felt unfriended, doored, housed,
demeaned by a mixed race of metaphors,
generalizations laced with the poison of truthiness.

We were hounded by welfare queens
with guns and religion, Mexican rapists,
moochers and takers.

While in the near distance
a trumpet roused
a xenophobic, racist mob to life
within the safe space
of an imaginary wall.

Identify

—Dictionary.com's 2015 word of the year: Identity

She could pass
for black or white.
Sister Rachel chose
to be black because
you can be what you wanna be
in America. She was just
being herself. Who dat? Who dat?
I-G-G-Y
or Eminem who out raps
the brothers in *8 Mile.*
Or Bill Clinton
the first black president.
Not Barack who never appears
too black. Or Elizabeth Warren
who doesn't even look like an Indian!

Wait, didn't Gatsby choose
his identity?
Like Bey and Jay-Z?
Isn't Rachel free
to claim authenticity?
Like 50 Cent only
her wounds—too deep
for us to see—
the makeup, hair and tan,
accessories
like hair extensions

or a weave—
as a woman, Rachel knows
the meaning of slavery,
and she wears her shackles like jewelry.

Whipping Boy

> "You must always remember . . . the great violence upon the body."
>
> —Ta-Nehisi Coates,
> *Between the World and Me*

Someone has to pay for our sins.
Believe you me, we feel your pain.
Don't try to resist, you'll never win.
We all need to learn to behave.

Believe you me, we feel your pain,
but the scars don't show as much on you.
We all have to learn how to behave.
The police, they have a job to do.

The scars don't show as much on you—
when they tie you to the post, take it like a man.
The police, they have a job to do.
The snap and crack is what you understand.

They'll tie you to a post, so take it like a man.
The police are the messengers and the message is clear.
The snap and crack is a song you understand.
Do what you're told. Control your fear.

The police are the messengers and the message is clear.
Don't ever resist—you can't win.
Do what you're told. Control your fear.
Someone has to pay for our sins.

How to Make Meatballs

I learned to make meatballs from my neighbor Tony
who hired me as a short-order cook
for the greasy spoon he owned in Southie.
The dead man's shift, midnight to eight, was slow—
plenty of time to teach me what to do.

We tore Italian bread apart,
held the pieces beneath the faucet
and squeezed the water out.
We cracked eggs into a bowl
and mixed the wet bread
with the red ground beef, oregano, and salt.

The meatballs baked while I fried
eggs, bacon, and home fries
for the working girls and drunks
who stumbled in.

This was before Tony went away
for printing twenties in his basement,
before Joey broke in and stole our TV,
and the bank took their house.

Miss Maloney

A doll, my mother proclaimed,
after meeting Miss Maloney
the new fifth grade teacher.
Just out of Bridgewater State Teacher's College,
an eraser over five feet tall,
natural blond hair in a bun,
blue eyes in a field of freckles.
Smiling, she invited us
to set goals for the year.
At recess, our war council convened.
We aimed to make her cry
for being so pretty and perky.
Each day at ten as she stood at the board
explaining prime numbers
we swept our math books
off our desks and the thump
made her neck snap back.
Afternoons as she read us
her favorite books, we cracked
our #2 pencils in half in unison,
lined up at the sharpener
and cranked it till it whined.
When she lost her cool and yelled,
we laughed so hard we fell
off our chairs and rolled
on the chalk-dusted floor.
Just before Christmas, she let
her hair down and cried,
fists clenched in desperation

while we cheered.
When she returned after break
she vowed she'd finish the year
and that would be the end
of her aborted teaching career;
she was going back to school for business.
Walking home, we exclaimed,
"We did it!" and high-fived,
though what we did was far from clear.
The middle school had plans for us.
They broke us up.
And then they broke us down.

Idling

He was good with his hands;
my father could fix
a leaky faucet
or a squeaky hinge.
He'd take on projects
whenever he'd visit.
He always kept his tools
in the trunk of his car.
He liked to keep them handy
in case the dishwasher
refused to start
or the wires crossed in a lamp
or a screen slider
slid off the track.
He tried to teach me
how to wield a wrench
when I was young
and I was happy to crawl
beneath a car
to change the shoes,
or hover over an engine
and with his guiding hand
adjust the idle.
But my mind was always
elsewhere—thinking
of Holden's phonies
or Nick's river
or Emily's eternity
and the way words sounded
when you put them together
and turned them over
in your mind.

Old Enemies

Let's not forget
the shock treatments
prescribed by her doctor
to temper her rage . . .

I have no memory
of her hitting me
though my sisters insist
she hit them
repeatedly. I do wonder
where the anger comes from
with it's low growl
and musky smell.
I keep it chained out back,
mostly, though it does get out
from time to time.

Of course I remember
her cruelty—
discarding the beautiful scarf
my sisters bought her for Christmas,
saying how disappointed
she was in them.

And the fights between us—
My mother and I snapping at each other,
screaming toe to toe!

Other times she was all smiles
for me—her favorite.
Maybe it was my brother and sisters

who got the brunt of it—
Jack, who fled to northern Maine
and never came back,
not even for the funerals.
While my sisters remained
close as cubs
with their shared secrets
and a tendency to stretch the truth
until it snapped and I didn't know
what to believe. Now

my mother and father are dead.
I've mellowed with age—
the fights, road rage, assault
with a dangerous weapon
behind me like old enemies.

Call to the Furies

Someone had to avenge
those who were wronged.
Still, they might have let
sleeping dogs lie
left to their own devices
but once they joined hands
they were a force to be reckoned with
and the more they plotted
the madder they got
until they were furious—
justifiably so! No father
should ever sacrifice a daughter
for his ambitions, and no son
should murder his mother—
or madness will result.
Though a wife may have reason
to kill her spouse . . .

Over time, it became plain,
no one should break an oath
or make promises he never intends to keep.
Or threaten a rival with imprisonment—
especially a wife and mother!

So we pray their vengeance
will be swift and terrible.

American Dream

> "In the Will, work and acquire and thou hast chained the wheel of Chance."
>
> —Ralph Waldo Emerson,
> "Self-Reliance"

Maybe it's the little kingdoms keeping the country intact.
The ranch on Cape Cod with the two-car garage he built himself.
One summer with his son, he added the deck
that overlooks a panorama of conservation land.
His Harley crouches in the driveway

beside the cherry Dodge Ram truck, and undercover,
a '76 Trans Am. The camper squats on the grass.
This is what twenty years in the Marines and twenty years in construction
buys him, his wife, and two kids.

An American flag snaps to attention in the yard.
Country music plays while steaks spit and sizzle on the grill.
He sings "Proud to be an American" meaning every word.

His son and daughter run the restaurant he bought for them.
He knows what hard work is and that's a boon he'll bequeath to them.
In this kingdom by the sea he claims: you get out what you put in.

American Elegy

We called crazy
A kind of fun—
A visit to the zoo
We'd make at will—
Let the animals out!
Drugs were just the ticket.
Alcohol fueled the fire,
The fumes enough
To knock you out,
Or get you in.
Door is always open!
we'd say, Hey, ho.

Now we know
It's no joke—
the list of ODs
long, and getting longer.

Call it a psychotic break—
a fissure that runs
through the heart
of the country
like a crack in a skull.

And at the wheel,
one of us.

Gypsy Moth

Slinky caterpillars, fuzzy brown
and red-dotted fingers with half a dozen legs
drop from above onto your neck
and crawl down your shirt
in search of food. They remain
hungry even after denuding
every deciduous tree in sight
until the trunks stand naked
like skinny kids in the middle of summer.
Now they're stressed like the rest of us,
susceptible to fungus and disease.

Intelligent design profiles butterflies
with their sun-splashed yellow
and orange polka-dotted wings.
They could well be queens
or kings of their domain.
But what kind of god
would fashion gypsy moths?
Each stage of growth worse:
from egg to larva to pupa to moth.
Fecund females lay one thousand eggs
beneath the unsuspecting bark of trees.
You'd think their saving grace
might be that by summer's end
they die—thwacking into window screens
desperately searching like the rest of us
for the light. But no.
They'll be back again next year
to feast on our canopy.

Encomium for the God of Nothingness

> "Some people feel that Trump will bring the revolution immediately . . ."
> — Susan Sarandon, March 28, 2016

This is where we are—on the verge.
Just over the edge—chaos.
A singular cell, chains, guard dogs,
the fate that awaits the false prophets,
those secular televangelists,
radio talk show hosts, advisers
to the Lord of Misrule
who prey on their marks
for profit and power,
those masters of disjuncture
and dysfunction—the high priests
of deceit at whose altar
my fellow Americans worship,
from their knees to their feet,
roaring in crowds, mingling
in mobs, chanting within
invisible walls where
everyone's eyes mirror
exactly what they want to see,
while echoes repeat
only what they want to hear.

Ex-Nuns

You see them around—the ex-nuns,
reed-thin, gray hair cropped short.
Stoic in their Puritan garb,
Long-faded dresses from another era
hide their pale legs. They don't give a fig

about food, avoid the drink,
except for an occasional glass
of cheap wine. You might catch them
sneaking a smoke in the alley
behind the Catholic school where they teach.

Although they quit the convent
years ago, plagued by doubt,
they still wake at dawn
repeating the rosary
every blessed day.

Baker's Chocolate

You could smell the chocolate
wafting in the air, half
a mile from the factory in Lower Mills.
It made us smile as we walked home
from school to think of what
was going on behind those walls—

the building blocks of birthday cakes
and chocolate chips, brownies and hot fudge.
Now, of course, the factory is long gone.
Gone the way of steel, and shoes, and jeans.
Yet none of them, ever smelled so sweet.

Social Security

—Enacted in 1935

He never signed up
for Social Security, my grandfather,
a mechanic who ran a one-man garage
behind the high school.
The locals were loyal. They paid
in cash. It was hard to find
a good mechanic and he knew cars
inside and out—could name
what was wrong with his ear,
and he seldom overcharged.
He never drank until he got home
where he took his Seagram's neat.
A sentimental drunk, he liked to sing
Irish songs. My father learned
not to drink from him
and from my uncle Bobby
who loved whiskey and the horses.
He had a system, he claimed,
after a good day at the track,
but that was just before
his third and final heart attack.
Ten years after my grandfather
retired at sixty-five and died a month later
of heart failure. He didn't need
Social Security, though my grandmother
surely disagreed.

In the Dead of Winter in Somerville

Underneath the street,
beside the tracks,
between the trains,
an Asian woman—all angles,
few curves, removes her black cloak,
inserts her violin between her chin
and collarbone and launches into
"Paint it Black" by the Rolling Stones
that morphs into some wild, jazz/blues fusion,
and draws a crowd with raised eyebrows
and unexpected smiles.
We toss dollar bills
into the worn case at her feet.

When the train roars in,
she stops and bows and we clap.
Do you have a CD? someone calls.
She shakes her head.
She is older than I thought.
Her roots are gray.

I step onto the train
wondering how many years
it took to reach
that plateau of facility
with bow and strings.

How many others?
Artists, musicians, poets—
wear the cloak of anonymity.

The Tropical Forest in Franklin Park

I brought my five-year-old to the Tropical Forest
in the Franklin Park Zoo. We discovered
a lowland gorilla relaxing with her infant
in her lap. They didn't seem unhappy.
My son stood inches away, separated
by glass. He was beside himself
with glee. Outside, half a dozen males
swaggered around a small field
enclosed by a fence. Surely
they missed the rich jungles of Africa
embedded in their genetic memory.
Wasn't it longing I saw
in those deep-set, sensitive eyes?

Royal Rendezvous in August

Two monarch butterflies hook up in midair.
Not the mile-high club, these acrobats
tryst shamelessly just off the ground—
no net needed. The orange- and black-lined wings
flutter like Japanese fans
keeping them aloft in dizzying flight.

Why not alight on a butterfly bush
where they can relax?
What's the rush?
A one-minute stand
and they're off on their own.

A black-and-blue swallowtail
spies jealously on.
Better find a mate soon, friend.
It's August and the long flight
from Maine to Mexico
is coded into your being
like the patterns on your wings.

Heron

All wings and legs,
you take your stilted stance
atop a branch
that seems too thin
to bear your weight
yet there you stand
in search of fish.

It's only when you fly
your beauty is revealed.
You glide on air
like a skull on a lake—
legs trailing behind like oars.

Curveball

It was a slow curve—a big bender,

spinning against the trajectory

of the ball. It hung

at the apex

suspending

time

distorting space

like a full moon, while

I waited back on my heels

And when I went for it, it was

nowhere near where I expected it to be.

Riding

      The board turned downhill
          and I followed
              riding the bright
          crystalline glaze
              until my thighs
burned. I was somewhere
          between standing and sitting,
gliding while linking
          seemingly endless
S curves—
          running so fast
              I couldn't quite
catch up
          with myself
and when I hit the berm,
          I used my legs to spring
and caught
          nothing but air.

Found Poem from "Lava, Land, and Life Forms," Melissa Cronin

Lava

Cataclysmic power spewing hot lava,
sending plumes of smoke
and noxious gases into the air
as lava rumbles beneath the earth.

Irrepressible ecological unifier,
razing earth, to create
new microbes. Plants and animals
will follow. Lava thrives in the wake
of volcanic eruptions, in their violent,
mesmerizing beauty—harbingers
of soil, rich in nutrients and minerals.

Under the shadow of Mt. Vesuvius,
fig trees and grape vines
spring up like mushrooms
in the dark, loamy, volcanic soil.

The Hawaiian Ohia Lehua tree
among the black, basalt ash,
first to crop up after a volcano,
red flowers pushing through
new cracks in the lava—
living laboratories for evolution
once the lava cools.

We Support Our Troops

Why bother to bury the bodies?
We keep them stacked like cords of wood
in the back of our minds.
There's always room for more! you say,
trying to be helpful.
In times like these,
we need to support each other
like pylons hold up houses.
Yet many are unmoored—
bored out of their gourds.
"Let's get high!" they say
and pass around the opioids.

So Many Men

As the sun rises, so many men
rise from bed each day
longing for death.

As we brush our teeth
and spit in the sink,
we know death hides like a secret
in the pills behind the mirror.
And death shows his face
when we clean our guns,
the bullets—messengers
always ready to deliver the mail,
an announcement written in lead.

After dinner we reach for death,
who floats in bottles sitting in the cupboard
waiting to be downed in shots.
And death drives our car at night,
half asleep at the wheel,
gas pedal to the floor, lights off.

We like to keep death close by as we age
and wonder why we're still here.

Funeral at Sea

The ocean laps the streets with its tongue.
Our feet wet as cement.
Termites of salt eat the roads.
Nevertheless, we keep our heads up.
Don't pay it any mind, everyone says.

We drive SUVs for the clearance,
water running underneath like mice.
It streams into driveways
and seeps into basements,
soaking carpets till they smell
like cats caught in the rain.
As long as we can drive, we'll be okay, you say.

I say we will learn to swim with the fishes.
We will return to the sea
where we'll arrange our funerals.

Summer in Wellfleet

In summer when cars flood the roads,
I take the trails through the woods.
Underfoot, sand and beach grass,
in the air, pine and pollen.
A canopy of oak leaves overhead
blocks the sun. Robins skitter before me
as I walk, a flock of turkeys
scampers past. If I'm lucky,
I'll run across a doe
or a bushy-tailed fox.
Ladder-backed woodpeckers
type their enigmatic code
into the bark of trees
and squirrels perform circus acts—
flying from branch to branch
while chipmunks search below
for gypsy moths that parachute
from above. I like to walk
to kettle ponds and swim
until I forget
whatever it was
I had to do.

Cahoon Hollow

Last winter the ocean swallowed
two tons of sand, and cut
The Beachcomber's parking lot
in half. Call it erosion
if you like the word.
Words don't do justice
when the ocean redefines
the coastline.
Seals bob indifferent
to our concerns—
they have sharks
in their wake!
Meanwhile, we swim
close to shore.
Parents keep a wary eye
on kids who dare
waves to knock them down.
Moms and toddlers crawl like crabs
into tents that screen the sun.
Overhead, the sky so blue,
it breaks your heart.

Something's Not Right

—For Tony Judt

You have the feeling that something's not right.
We made a wrong turn somewhere back there.
If we could step back we might see the light.

I guess you could say that we've lost sight
of what's important and who we are.
You have the feeling that something's not right.

Once we had dreams; we knew what was right.
We knew where to look for a guiding star.
If we could step back we might see the light.

The world's upside down: day's become night.
If there's a way forward, it's no longer clear.
You have the feeling that something's not right.

Some are determined to rely on might,
but endless wars won't clear the air.
If we could step back we might see the light.

We can't let ourselves get mired in spite.
We can't live our lives based on our fears.
You have the feeling that something's not right.
If we could step back we might see the light.

Nevertheless

—For Elizabeth Warren

She was warned, given an explanation.
Nevertheless, she persisted. Understand,
there are rules of decorum in our nation.
She impugned the reputation of a man.

Nevertheless, she persisted. Understand?
She was clearly in violation of the rules.
She impugned the reputation of a man.
Maybe she should have to go back to school.

She was clearly in violation of the rules.
Like others before her she didn't understand.
Someone should have to go back to school.
Like Rosa Parks, she was taking a stand.

Like others before her, she couldn't understand.
Take Susan B. Anthony demanding the vote.
Or Barack Obama saying, Yes, we can.
They promised change; they gave us hope.

Well, they were warned, given an explanation.
Nevertheless, they persisted. Understand,
there are people in charge who take us for fools.
Maybe it's time we changed the rules.

Ghost Bikes

—For Amanda Phillips

In case you missed the story
of the barista struck by a truck
in Inman Square in Cambridge,
a ghost bike painted white
occupies a corner, roses
and lilies sprouting from the frame.

White bikes lean against
metal poles, from Detroit
to Boston, Amsterdam
to Seattle. Some are twisted
and broken; others
look like new. They carry
the memories
of riders blindsided,
doored, cut off by cars,
buses and trucks—seats empty
where a person once was,
handlebars hands-free,
brakes untouched.
Signs say: Cyclist Struck Here,
as if we didn't know.

As if we didn't know what happens
when a woman on a bike
swerves around
an open car door

to find a truck
closing in on her
like a ship
colliding with a dock,
shattering the dream she had
for med school, marriage, kids,
a condo in Cambridge.

Unlike your everyday spirits,
these ghost bikes are not invisible.
We can see them
with our own eyes—
stark and skeletal,
bleached as bones by the sun.

On the Train

Rubber straps shaped like nooses
hang from steel rods in subway trains.
Lucky for us, they're too small
for human heads. Instead, we hang on
for balance when the train lurches
and careens around a bend.
It can be hard to keep your balance
in America where the politicians
steal us blind and line
the pockets of their friends.
Keep your eyes open.
These are the same souls
that hanged nineteen women in Salem.
It turns out we are easily bewitched,
deluded by events beyond our control:
random fires, crop failures, seizures,
assassinations, terrorist attacks all demand
retribution. Someone has to pay
for our sins and when there are no witches
to be found, there are negroes
to be hanged. Like negroes and Asians,
all Arabs look alike. A little shock
and awe is good for us. Troops
protect the oil and drones
are our missionaries. Meanwhile
we hang on for dear life.
You can understand our need
for opioids, guns, and a savior.
Someone who promises
a return to the life we never had.

The Last Game

When you die you will slide
under the tag at home,
dust rising in the air.

On the Outer Cape

One hundred miles south of Boston
where the Cape curls up
like a dog's tail,
a gazillion stars
redefine the night.

We've stepped out onto the porch
to search for falling stars
which aren't stars at all
but meteorites—
white streaks of cosmic dust—
flaming out like dreams at dawn.

In August they announce
the coming end of summer.
Meanwhile, in the garden,
fireflies surprise us
with their ethereal presence
and the miracle
of bioluminescence.

Maybe it's the timing
that makes us savor
these sacred gifts.

Permissions

"The Black Paintings," "The Last Game," *Chronogram*; "Crossing Guard," *The Grey Sparrow Journal*; "Junkyard of Broken Dreams," *American Journal of Poetry*; "Limbo," *The Comstock Review*; "The Lottery," "Powder Blue," *War, Literature and the Arts*; "The Poetry Motel," *Poetry Motel*; "In the Poetry Motel," *The Prose-Poem*; "Make America Great Again," *The New Renaissance*; "Talking Trees," "Advertisement Paid for by the Poetry for American Expression PAC," *Cognoscenti*, WBUR; "Sail Away," *Wilderness House Literary Review*; "American Elegy," *Constellations*. "Sigh," *The Paddock Review*; "Death to Poetry," *Muddy River Poetry Review*; "For My Mother," *FishFood Magazine*; "Pi," "Gliding," "Maid Pouring Milk," (Editor's Pick) "March," *The Aurorean*; "Rouault's Painting of Christ," *The Ekphrastic Review*. "Funeral at Sea," *New Southerner*; "Downy Woodpecker," *Blueline*; "Summer in Wellfleet," *Poetry Sunday*, WCAI; "Dumb Luck," *Tell-tale Inklings*. "Hammock," "Idling," "Gypsy Moths," *The Pinyon Review*; "Curveball," *Hobart*; "The Crossing Guard," Boston City Hall Exhibit, Mayor's Poetry Program; "Lava," *Meat for Tea: The Valley Review*; "Angel Falls," *Valley Voices*; "Pilloried," *High Shelf Magazine*; "Nine First Fridays," "How to Make Meatballs," *Nixes Mate Review*; "Something's Not Right," *The Deronda Review*; "Heron," *Tiny Seed Literary Journal*; "On the Outer Cape," "Miss Maloney," "In the Dead of Winter in Somerville," *Cognoscenti*, WBUR; "Old Enemies," *Constellations*; "Ghost Bikes," *The Broadkill Review*. "Pinch Me," *Gabriel's Horn Anthology;* "Nevertheless," *Colere;* "Encomium for the God of Nothingness," *Into the Void;* "Kiss," "Social Security," Gival Press: *ArLiJo Magazine*; "Gypsy Moths," "Hunting Mushrooms with Mina," *The HitchLit Review*.

About the Author

ED MEEK writes poetry, fiction, articles, and book reviews. *High Tide* is his fourth book of poems. *Luck*, a collection of his short stories, came out in 2017. He has been published in *The Sun, The Paris Review, The North American Review, Cream City Review, The Boston Globe Magazine,* and NPR's *Cognoscenti,* among others. He teaches creative writing at Cambridge Center for Adult Education, helps adults prepare for the high school equivalency exam, and in his spare time, walks his dog Mookie.

www.ingramcontent.com/pod-product-compliance
Lightning Source LLC
Chambersburg PA
CBHW052117110526
44592CB00013B/1642